PICTOGRAPH

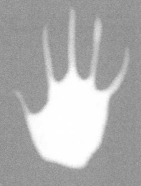

PICTOGRAPH

MELISSA KWASNY

poems

MILKWEED EDITIONS

Published 2015 by Milkweed Editions
Printed in Canada
Cover design by Mary Austin Speaker
Cover photograph by Melissa Kwasny
Author photo by Bryher Herak
15 16 17 18 19 5 4 3 2 1
First Edition

Milkweed Editions, an independent nonprofit publisher, gratefully acknowledges sustaining support from the Bush Foundation; the Jerome Foundation; the Lindquist & Vennum Foundation; the McKnight Foundation; the National Endowment for the Arts; the Target Foundation; and other generous contributions from foundations, corporations, and individuals. Also, this activity is made possible by the voters of Minnesota through a Minnesota State Arts Board Operating Support grant, thanks to a legislative appropriation from the arts and cultural heritage fund, and a grant from the Wells Fargo Foundation Minnesota. For a full listing of Milkweed Editions supporters, please visit www.milkweed.org.

Library of Congress Cataloging-in-Publication Data
Kwasny, Melissa, 1954-
  [Poems. Selections]
  Pictograph : poems / Melissa Kwasny. -- First edition.
    pages ; cm.
  ISBN 978-1-57131-462-8 (softcover) -- ISBN 978-1-57131-908-1 (ebook)
  I. Title.
  PS3561.W447A6 2015
  811'.54--dc23

                          2014031512

Milkweed Editions is committed to ecological stewardship. We strive to align our book production practices with this principle, and to reduce the impact of our operations in the environment. We are a member of the Green Press Initiative, a nonprofit coalition of publishers, manufacturers, and authors working to protect the world's endangered forests and conserve natural resources. Pictograph was printed on acid-free 100% postconsumer-waste paper by Friesens Corporation

I.

II.

III.

PICTOGRAPH

I.

Prior to writing as a form of possession what lights and shadows swept the walls.

SARAH GRIDLEY

OUTSIDE THE LITTLE CAVE SPOT

The opening to the world is lopsided, irregular, dipping down like a lock of hair over someone's eye. Outside the cave: liquid gold, silver. Inside: as if flesh had been scraped off. Of the many ancient virtues, hope is the one you almost forgot. Limestone so dry and jagged, so pockmarked, it could cut your skin. It stops you. Like a clock stops: you are here. From inside, you see that you are often unkind to others. You shake hands without taking off your gloves. There is a motor of living water outside your ear. Little socket, the earth is frozen, cold and skinny and breaking down. You could lean out and lend your warmth to it. You sit here and the cries are muffled. You worry how, in the matter of a single letter reversed, a bit of food during a fast, a shade too dark for the sky-paint, sacred can turn scared and cause harm. This is how large you are. A thumbprint in a cliff. How much you are asked to keep in mind.

PICTOGRAPH: AVALANCHE MOUTH

We didn't know what we were seeing, and so, saw less. Red lightly painted over the surface. They showed themselves like the animals do, only in certain light. It was an empty place we visited, and then they filled it. The coaxing of figures, as if out of a dream, from the corners of dream into the open: handprints, finger-lines, a turtle. Meander outside the area of recent spalls. Dark and cold this time of year, in the canyon, and we were sullen, increasing the severity of where we are. A crazy mean lost culture, blue going in the wrong direction. Always interfering with something sacred still going on. Deer-sex in the interior: one must move by touch. The walk-through pictograph in the making. Ever since we were born, we could imagine these still and silent fields. Deer positioned on top of hay mounds in the safe zones.

PICTOGRAPH: THE RED DEER PLACE

Close to the river, rain-clear near its shore: seven doe, rose-orange. A mother with a fawn. One starburst. A hundred tally marks. A kind of feather. Clear water, red lacquer of the bare dogwood branches, the shale muted, mixed, spirit tempered with blood. Rock-blood, which is a flower shade, more silent, safer. Your mother is entering a timelessness on the edge of death. A light source so distant we feel auxiliary. Yet a loud thrumming of our ears against the gates. Why do whitetail deer have a white tail that could so easily betray them? Does it bind them like knots in a rope at night or in the confusion of flight from harm? The white is not so bright in the broken tines of hoarfrost, the penciled-in trunks of aspen that fall in lines like faults or fences, yet these look like deer bodies, too. It is perhaps the heathering, the empty space between the colors. A fading language that might be bridge to our existence here.

THE SHAMAN'S CAVE

Up in long steps through heat to heat, each tree a station where we recover. O, un-diseased trees, who hold a place for us. That the earth was such a place. Place your hand there. Or rather, there were pools here, but they are dry now, smeared with guano. From this nest, Thou directs. The cold winds leap. Our valley, murderous, far below. Unnatural green of our truck and of our pasturage. Is this the state of our interior—barren? Is this where the waxwing song—plummets? All people still dream. The thresholds appear, arcs stained with hematite, red ochre. Which give way to zigzags and stars. Until the line that divides the world in two snaps. Until we lose all courage before this cause. From deep within, something tosses the tops of the highest trees. We are without shields. Intrinsic lack of the right weapon: possible bear, possible star figure, possible god.

CHICKADEES AND THEIR ALLIES

The flower chart expresses in concise and graphic form the general lines of evolution from the ancestral buttercups, silverberry, sow thistle, goosefoot. The larger rocks crowd together in the downward stream. Water buffalo, bottom-feeding with their snouts. Patterned with lichen, the shadow of a chartreuse beard. They say, you, wading there, are like an ant, a speck of dust. You, who are busy and then gone. And the cloud cover? Eccentric. Who rose at six to paint a second coat of ocher on the walls. A staging ground, where we eat our lunch, scatter tobacco. I am trying to find out what bird accompanied us from the cave, a black-and-white one, but was it wagtail or eastern kingbird? Enigmatic birds, like people, like rocks—who knows what are their shields or what protects them? Four grosbeaks land out of nowhere, like dried leaves, with citrine veils. I mistake the raindrops on aspen limbs for buds.

THE SENTIENCE OF ROCKS

Take the origin of this stillness. Divide it into bits. What is form but the reining in of desire? As we age, we drape less. Charcoal peppered across our caps. Suddenly, we have microscopes for eyes. We complain of our "loose habits," by which we mean we drink and smoke. Our bodies won't stay long, although our bones can. Surely, we will be given time to explore the diverticula of the heart. The long, most beautiful summers coming to an end. We sense the shadow-bearing figures, day and night, mixed as they are. We might be stage. We might be inconsequential. We begin to sleep close to the sound of the creek. We stockpile our warmth for the others. Do our dreams prepare us for our eventual deaths? There is no time there. Therefore, there is no breath. Small area of dots and hand-smears outside the rose-orange wash of blood. They are watching us from there, Pilgrim. Whoever they are.

BEING QUARTZ

Parchment upon parchment. Hoofprints across the snow. A thousand cracks in a glassy ceiling. There is light there, the windows double-paned, the doors shuttered tight. Dirt can't get in, can only scuff the surface. Even the most strenuous hiddenness must unfold and die. Is death then an extreme condition of exteriority? What is inside grown exceedingly out? The animals have come down. I can hear them roaming, though I can't place them. A slow process, marked by indirection and great lull. I read that the path to the underworld passes through a region of ice. I read, "the alert and autistic ends of the mind's spectrum." The shaman's cache is not in the cave but inside the rock walls, where she keeps her toolbox, her maps and set of instructions. Where she calls out the vowels, open and endless. Where she watches as her teeth and lips close.

PICTOGRAPH: POSSIBLE SHIELD-BEARING FIGURE

To the phrase "We mean you no harm," I have added, "We wish you well." How the day trims the night with blue trade cloth. How the night offers long-distance bells. And the wine-makers appear to mix the waters. Lately, the rivers have begun to talk, in their loudspeaker voices, as if projected. As if they were speaking from a crack that opened deep inside the cliff, as if they were placed there like a feather in a book. Yesterday, I had one of the Old Days. As they say, my solitude was extended. An implied but un-depicted ground line. An abstract foothills tradition. The sound of rivers can lead me back there, to what I am being carried along to find. Their lives, this one, a kind of drowning. Imagine it summer. The rock shelter is dry. Scrape of chert. Chirr of insects in the fescue. The earth alive in ways I am not. Dead in ways beyond my reckoning.

PICTOGRAPH: HELLGATE CANYON

Not a place to "house" the dead but a place for them to appear. Red ocher, made of rock, bound with the living: egg, fat, urine. In other words: wave the paint stick near the surface. Feather the incense in. What would spirit be inside the earth if we could see it? Foothold, finger-hold, grasping onto the bare shelves, its steps trailing down to the ancient rivers. Foxglove, how the spirit hides. Its carapace, the cliff. Does it resemble the human body, loosely woven, like cheesecloth? Or is it dense, dark grit on a ledge? I wonder if they were scared, if they were children, men or women. Chained in lines that seem knotted even as they stretch out. Note the extensive scratches on what could only be a torso. The wind, the trees cry after them with open mouths. The saddest piece of music ever written.

PICTOGRAPH: STAR BEING CAVE

Womb of earth and we, its organs. It is bone-dry, now dead. To run our hands over its sides would be to scrape them. Lice-filled nests, broken shells with inner seams of blood, guano pooling like oil on the ledges. Flicker and pigeon feather, dirt and scat in tiny chains of pellets, rat or squirrel, some fur-bearing creature hunting eggs. But if there were a fire, if we crouched by it in the night, walls drawn with stars and humans who resemble stars or birds, the cave would come alive, by which I mean the lower kind rush out, the eagle walk with its wings lifted so they don't drag. Its eye, a predator's eye. Graffiti and beer cans, the deep ruts cut from a truck in spring, the curators who chiseled out the central pictograph and then left—couldn't they see it? How it ties us to the past? The cave has elbows. The cave breathes and counts its breaths, its cavities filling up with light and dust and allergens.

CAVE SYSTEM

Eerily, in false light, the ceremonial octaves go dim, lit by a fluorescent bulb, which casts no shadow. Stalactites. Stalagmites. Snow White and the seven dwarves. Our tour guide points out Rudolf, the red-nosed reindeer. We bring our noise to it, our wish to be entertained. Children touch where they are asked not to touch. Adults worry the particulars of their private worlds. Room where form is generated, rum-dark and smudged. Overstock room where the cycles end. Water carved out this cave—Montana an inland sea—and since then, our matters have taken precedence. Room where our prayers do not find fertile soil. Where calcium fails from overreaching. What if we had moved through it, instead, as a silence? No, slower, as if we were its blood? If we had acknowledged what a rare thing it is to be here? That the weather held for generations, hospitable to us.

PETROGLYPH: BIRD WITH SPEECH SYMBOL

Gestures in the willow limbs: chimestones, plummets. Where there is land birds will come back with grasses. Speak to everything. What kind of echo chamber can you create? The fire still burning low in the basement. Or, as I did, spend an hour outside under the wide brim of sky which scientists—scientists, what an old-fashioned word!—say no artificial spectrum can match. On the radio, a man is speaking of light, how it enters predominantly through the eye, but it has also entered behind the knee, igniting its transformation of the cells. The house is closed. The walls opaque. And then the windows, the doors begin to glow. One sees them now, can go to them and open them. Scintilla: the least trace. To make light of matter. The tamer birds, their shadow-worts on the ground. Like seed-casks, like the aftereffect of laughter.

PICTOGRAPH: BIZARRE ANTHROPOMORPH,
OFTEN WITH INTERIOR BODY DECORATIONS

Note left foot with interior spiral. Note the torso, storehouse of resins and gums. We have been here before, counting as we step down. Counting: tool of the magicians. Perhaps the Hopi are right, that we emerged from the earth, like bears. Perhaps that is why we carry the earth-jars inside us. We recognize our companions as they pass on the left. By drift of sage, an iridescence of throat armor. The gay men have cues, a plain or plaid bandana, in the front pocket or the back, as the gangs do. Erratic: the field of our remains. A scientist on the radio says that, contrary to past belief, the damaged brain can learn to heal itself. We can take back our pogroms, we could pray the blind to see, perhaps two leaders, enemies, who will stop now. Thoreau died whispering "Indians" and "buffalo," it is said. We do sometimes get to choose our lives. Set in motion, as it has been explained to me.

PICTOGRAPH: INTERIOR BODY DECORATIONS

Your nipple, pierced and threaded with a golden bar. Next to it, the cancer they cut away. I place my hand on my heart and then on yours. This brings tears to your eyes and mine. Mattress springs buried in the garden plot. A tree at the groin. Under which the animals threaten and sleep, sleep and threaten. Of course, we are attached to the personal narrative. We are the luckiest people alive! The dropped threads of the bare alder limbs that from a distance look like smoke. The prettiness of the herbs the winds bring. Our days are luxurious, coffee ground fine, the color of mink, after dinner. How fear can still blind us to these things. Look at all these ribstones. Note the extra hands and feet. How could we have lived with our thresholds so un-entangled? You arrive. You kiss me. Then, we carry your things in, which always include handheld wands and public fringes.

MY FIRST ERMINE

The guide says they mate in summer but implantation is delayed, a total gestation of almost a year. Little ermine, slow to catch, like a flame. Like the photos of the young woman at Abu Ghraib posing next to corpses with her gesture: thumbs up. Mothers, start again, remember your place in this. The earth is softening. The war is still on. Hello, the pines are all tail. Changeling of the season, mark our betrayal now. A bomb amid the people at the holy shrine. It is time to calm the children. To spread petals on the old. Seed packets: a ceremonial prosody. Cooped up, as they say, with the body and its obsessions, laying our pale eggs, with the rest, in wet straw. A chill when the door is opened. But more and more, days in the sun. The ermine trills inside the woodpile and shows his white face once. I take away the dog who is barking at it. What is the ritual? Mothers, tell us again. At night, only moon, visit your invisible ones.

PICTOGRAPH: BIRD SITE, MAZE DISTRICT

This morning and at twilight, the ouzel frames the night, singing *If I have searched more for beauty than for love*. . . . My Paraclete, my advisors: green syrup of shade, alder limbs falling silver from their common trunk. My world, my shield, my rain-colored stems, and the body, how it made it through the winter, shot half full with war-dust and rot. Site 1: Anthropomorph with Large Hands and Horns. Site 2: A Tree Extends Upward from the Middle Hand. There are engravings in caves, some 10,000 years old, someone's initials and dates of victory spray-painted over them. We recognize a figure, a brother, a twin, who is punished for our disabilities, our own strangeness. We are removed from our families or we remove ourselves. How will we remember the mountain? That the wine-dipped fringe of catkins appears overnight. That the aspen twigs are softened, like bread in milk.

PICTOGRAPH: SHIELD WITH LUNAR ECLIPSE

Milk in the eyes. Whatever the moon sees, she nourishes. The other way of being we have turned our backs on: the over-grown path, the door strangled with vines, the jar of sticks somehow connected to my grandfather, who is himself perhaps a sign. How we insist on being unhinged from each other. In the dream, I went shopping for something to drink. All the drinks told me why they wouldn't fit me: beer was too large, wine wrong and soiled, gin pretty and vacant. Whiskey, a pair of tight heels. How to keep one's attention on the vision? A poet writes that the three most important questions are dawn, noon, and midnight, without which the day *proceeds without punctuation*. Noon, unchanging, too close and bright to see, too still without the ornaments of god. We live between the other two as between the sound of two streams. The moon resembles a painting done in bronze. I am getting warmer, darker, aware of having limbs, aware of something trying to straighten them.

THE CLOUD EXERCISE

An earth that was beautiful has entered its death throes, beneath the gaze of its
fluttering sisters, in the presence of its insane sons.

—René Char

Darkened slate and gray skies + leaves = blue. What is the wind-dog? Flowers with rain. Rain with flowers. We were reading about the pictographs. We were entering the clouds. Our dear *fluttering sisters*. Do you remember the black-necked stilts, their pink legs knee-deep in spill? Their nights, so active, so down to earth? The clouds in their attic bedroom, filled with lightning? Like insects that lift and scatter as our legs move through tall grass, the animals surreptitiously rise up the timbered slopes away from us. What shall we call this? Tragic passage in the summer heat? Or loop of their vanishing through flag and fringe, low to the ground, the tiny, trodden ones? Whenever my friend plucks a weed—toadflax, knapweed, leafy spurge—he asks it to come back as something better. Even mullein, which is known to heal, which is invasive.

MY PICTOGRAPH

This is what I would have drawn, an ocher-colored bird, wings tucked, almost purple crown or glyph above its head. Orientation, my friend. We help each other. It is the sun that brings us color. No water and no sun here, only a fire and a few people painting. The rest of us are smoke, standing on the scaffolding. If we could draw what we are, draw the inside out to be displayed, and later, as we move out onto the plains . . . look, here is a rock that you found for me. Wind high up, wind's sharp leaves. One way pointing, one blocking the exit. That we can talk to each other in this way. Inside each life is a death. Inside the earth there are caves, the walls charcoal, sand, myrrh-of-the-body. Today, I am burning the piles of green cottonwood slash, the sap throaty, pungent, sour as ale. Soon, a branch will crack and everything will fall into its place. Later, I will wash the ash from my clothes.

LOST PICTOGRAPH

The light darkened, stained to the thin color of Chinese tea, then lost its muscle and unraveled. Dust covering the shine we lost on surfaces. We lost, too, some will, never our strong suit. Disturbing, the children who, once we have mentioned the word "grenade," cannot think about anything else. We lost: our facility to stand in front of people, prepare ourselves for the event. While the others wound strips of deer hide round the feather stems. We lost: a comfort alone in our own house. On national shame: you don't see it much here. Weed scratching against weed on the dry plains. We lost two days to the snow geese, driving to them for hours, then watching their singular white drift. The way a flock becomes a line that turns cursive. We know what winter is: isolate, long, searching futilely for a nest for our blue eggs. Almost losing our memory that there are leaves.

II.

Earth, isn't this what you want:
invisibly to arise in us?

RAINER MARIA RILKE

PETROGLYPH: THE BLUE HARE

I can't tell if it's the wind over its surface or the light, but the snow rings. As if the roots of the flowers were stirring here. I make a path with my boots. I make a sign and I receive. Light is a feeling. I feel light. Then, there is a memory of how long it has been with me: all those dawns, the drift of lemon scarves. Who was I? All those selves never recovered. Behind me, the blue-filled tracks of farewell. The light humanity invents is inelegant—broken or scrambled—not like this morning, which pours forth in strong lines. I should enlarge the bedroom windows. Do away with the deck. The goal: to live the interior into the open. With the exception of the hare, all species dig their own separate entrances from the subterranean world. The place of sensitivity may move from eye to ear. Listen: the slowly altering rock, the cave, the path, the flower, the mountain, and beyond.

THE CRUX OF WEATHER CHANGING

After a week of shimmering, the cottonwood leaves turn and enter the body triumphant. Then the snow comes, two feet of it. How this time of year makes a world, and the world makes a room, and we are here, in close proximity to perception. Driving at night, snow swirling across the road, as if we were skimming thin ice, speeding above a barely concealed current. A woman is losing her hold on the earth. She tells the same story again, throwing her hands in the air as if to fling ashes into the sea, to show me how the big dog knocked her back. If it is true that we abjure serenity, not that we have learned to disdain peace, it is because the measure of a good life is one of tension—light already departing when we wake. Old friend again back from your separate journey, let us celebrate in some quiet, handheld way. The bare limbs are white now, the heartwood dark, the center of the changing tree still gold.

YOU WAKE CLAIMING THERE ARE EIGHT
KINDS OF LIGHT

Into my beloved room, loved for the light, clean and pale and distant, the morning beds shyly its winter-wings. You have been dreaming. You are half in dream still. If only we were a species that just observes. Sun? I ask you. Yes. Moon? No. Sun. Photosynthesis. Me. I had been thinking about the Herzog movie, how the men kept stuffing dynamite into the ice, in order to see further into the Antarctic, compelled to stick their noses into everything. *Northern lights*, you say, surfacing. *Rainbows. The light at the bottom of the sea.* You sink back into sleep, flicking off switch after switch, locking doors, diverting the water to the tin-house, a sorrow, as if all were used up. *Outer space*, you had said. *The light at solstice.* So much snow across town the roofs are caving in. So much snow one might think it a cloud-filled day. But surely there must be more, I keep thinking.

THE SPECTRUM

Lit hallways between the unlit rooms on the slope under fir and pine. If I were a painter, I would have no need to name the colors. I would mix them, as Sarah does when she writes that garden rain is *a wand of soaked fire*. I would say hyacinth with drift of morning sky in the ditches. Sashes tied behind my back. I would cast a higher order from this worrying, the picking apart without respect: every bone x-rayed, every wing banded. I hear birdsong I haven't heard before, scalloped and filigreed, ask it to come closer, and it becomes two birds on two trees, solitaires, restive and furtive. At the time he divided the rainbow, Newton's vision was so poor he needed an assistant's help. To align with the intervals in the octave, the number of days in a week, he added orange and blue to equal seven. The solitaires are not solitary. They live in the light, where they imperceptibly bleed into each other. Mourning dove of the shadows. Lichen splashed across the rocks.

A TALK OF WINDOWS

Here is your day in front of you, frost on the vetch, and light finds its purchase on yellow walls. *Put on your rainbow colors,* the Navajo poem begins. You would like to dress for it, to dress the part. Drawing curtains open, one of the pleasures in life. Glass the color of a winter birthstone. What you see and what you hear, mostly water, sometimes rain. Small creatures chewing the pansies off their stems. Reflection: what is missing in most people's lives, a quality we find difficult to practice. You think of it as looking inward, reconnecting with your depth, yet moon reflects the life the sun shines on it. It shines it back as moon, as what we know as moon, white peach wrapped in newsprint, grouse whortleberries now gone, habitation floor of bottle flies now hatching. A window, when not a mirror, is time-factored thought, as well as a record that can be shattered. Night window. Day window. Frame with three trees. Designated craft room of the senses.

SIGN WITH CONVERGENT NESTED ELEMENTS

We are afraid the lovely scarves we bought at the Italian market will suddenly seem frayed in this northern light. Mother in the nursing home, chocolate smeared on her fleece pants. We make do with our offerings, spread out upon her bed: oranges, small brightnesses, toys with moving parts, the fog, a white river, our cold hands. It is said that knowledge comes like this, out of a cloud of unknowing. Emergent, the line of trees. Two or three blades of grass. Not an illusion, a word that I once used. Sometimes things shine forth with their own magnitude. Brushstroke of the mountain above the bank. As one ages, it seems to me, one begins to separate from the body. One sees its frailties, its needs at a remove. Dimly lit, not important to return to. This life gives us earth then turns us aside in sleep. We have sleep built in, a counter-shade, zinc colored.

WHAT STARLIGHT HAS BECOME
IN THE MOVING TREES

You say you've learned from observing old people. They reserve grief for their closest few. A deer's gaze: the path not the path-side grasses. We are standing on the brick sidewalk, by your still un-leafed hedge. April sky, color of drowned lilacs. What will be hardest is to lose friends, I say. We have both already lost one or two. I say friends, and the sun seems to come closer. An intimate, I remember, her last name suddenly on a storefront sign where I had stopped the car after driving around lost in that strange town. *Bear in mind / you are little holding a big person's glass.* I am scared about how nothing stays new. Watching men eating ice cream almost always makes me want to cry. It's your shameless pleasure. How you had wanted to show me the shops. Like a vase on a wooden table when a train comes through, a kind of trembling sings the vacancies in the brush. What starlight has become in the moving trees.

HOSPICE

The psychic talks to your mute brother in plain, slow speech, yet she is a white rhododendron when she listens. He tells her what he likes, the strings of colored lights, the row of abstract paintings above his bed. *"Hope" is the thing with feathers*, Emily Dickinson wrote. Despair, *the Hour of Lead.* Anger is a pitiable power, weaker. Yesterday, I heard on the radio that loneliness can pollute the lungs, that it is as destructive to the body as smoking. Your house is busy with aid workers, shift exchanges, the little dog. Your feeders with six western tanagers. So much bigger than us, the hand of god. Today, it waves over the roof tiles, which is to say the house fills. The way the sight of snow can soften us. All creatures gather around someone acting in a sacred manner—and serving suet. They perch in the garden, so bright they invite counting. They perch in the grass, fat with fat.

THE HERON ROOKERY

White pelicans practice their slow maneuvers against the clouding sky, their drag calming waves and wind below. If our movements could make a difference, if our conscious breath could bring peace, our voices used only for reconciliation of the bitterns and the dark of reeds? The boats settle into the current as we let the oars rest. If we cry, it would be like sitting in this shade. Be blue, be silent, be straw and rain, be dignified and gray, be alone. Shouldn't every act be painstaking? Shouldn't we take extreme care in all we do? Sunk in meditation, ignoring our bright crafts, each heron stares out at nothing, in its pitchforked nest, each tree a condominium of half a dozen. How can they stand it, these solitaries, intolerant of noise, constructing these ancient cities where they give birth. Heron at the opening in its black-spotted silk, flashing its silver mirrors from deep inside. And I, who hated family life as a child.

KAYAK

We glide like swans into their habitat: aeries in the slanted trees. We go further than we have ever gone before, past the lone heron, a storm cloud dissipating after rain, and the lesser guards with their brown mates, their ecstatic trill. It offends the forest to speak too loudly or sing there. The reindeer people do not say good-bye but slip quietly away, and when they enter someone's tent, they stand in the doorway, waiting for their presence gradually to become known. Mergansers, one ocher next to the obvious white and black male, the two flying so close that she seems his shadow. What you think is a drowned chassis is, in fact, a nesting crane. It lifts off its straw bale and slowly walks away, stiff legs robotically dismantling. How easily, how unconsciously we can disturb. Not like the herons, whose wide-winged eruption low over the marsh is a shout we hear only with vision. We have memorized the poem about the vixen, the blackbird, and the moon. Perhaps they sense that in us, and do not startle.

THE ROSS GIANT CEDARS

Bead lilies amid the ferns. Water trickling through moss. Until now, they have lived their whole lives without us. In the slot of light the mountains left for them. A wooden cabinet with scented drawers. A pool of land at the bottom of the familiar. They are large as a giant's work boot, a Salish canoe for twenty-six, though it could not fit in these multiple streams but needs the ocean. We gaze up through the boughs as one does through the open-work crochet of sleep, the feather costumes both world and dream try on. I read that Joyce could survive having schizophrenia, while his daughter could not, because he was a genius. There was room for every voice. His genius, he could assign a role to each of them. The cedars whisper and cough, always gruff, but in subterranean communication with each other. Five hundred years they have been living, the grove much older still. Huge pumps forcing rain four stories up. To get lost would be easy, is part of the tale, and we almost do, with no signage and no memory of the loop we've taken.

COUNTING THE SENSES

To sense the dead around us, in places where they are attached, or to sense past lives within the present one. To sense the presence of birds or animals on the roadside in the dark, or the moods of birds or animals, let alone people. There are tribes who can orient, even in the fog, naming the direction, east or west, that they are facing. There is the ability to see through lies, to feel an enemy at your back, to detect poison without taste, to dowse for water. You are up before dawn, walking the shore, picking up broken bits of plastic and shell. To sense in ever-refined levels the dissipating cloud-layers of oneself, what Ezra Pound named an "aristocracy of emotion." In the spruce copse near the confluence, you left your hair. Last night, we played Scrabble. My first word was divine. You added an s to it, doubling your score. In this very room, fourteen years ago, you turned over and found the lump. Your hand rose to it, as if guided by a sense of love.

LOW TIDE PICTOGRAPH, MADE OF SEAWEED, WITH HEADDRESS, DANCING

Ezra Pound wrote of terraces *the colour of stars*, like this backwash of tide on wet sand. Seaweed: jade cellophane. White-crowned sparrows in the beach grass, repeating each morning *we-we-we forget*. A woman appears on the shoreline. She does what humans do, bends at the waist, picks things up, examines them, and puts them down again. Much like the raven or western gull. Remember that you are a gesture, a salt and water drum, in resonance with the personal and the ancestral. If there really is more than one species of hominid on the earth—the visionary, the gentle, the agrarian, or those at war, *people of the truth and people of the lie*—how do we separate ourselves now? Four figures, in the distance, twirl and pose, a hieroglyph we can read from left to right. Queen on her throne of driftwood, a tangled buoy in one hand, the other dragging behind her the reins of kelp.

GEOGRAPHY LESSON

Where is your community located? Limping and soiled, without access to art or trees, one can see how the people are dragged down. *Does it have a shape?* Rainstorms, field trips, snow days, what catches like the deer's fur on the barbs. When the need is not so great, decadence. *What does the landscape look like?* But the need for beauty is a real need, berry baskets made of cedar, tule, using corn husks, bear grass for contrast. *Does it touch any water?* A swath of darkness amid the street lights, which indicates the river, the cottonwood trees far above it, masonic in feigned light. Water-fields of shooting stars, nerve endings. *What is the weather like?* Immense mandala-like star quilt. White sunflower appliqué. *Who lives there?* Ruby flash of the grosbeak's scarf: throat armor. Wild penstemon: blue sugar tossed against dust. *What animals live there?* Where the designs come from when we close our eyes.

THE EMERGING FIELD OF IMAGE THEORY

It is a huge thing to live. Inevitable, my neighbor says. While the pine beetles kill the pine forest that surrounds us. Gather your important papers, your painting of the lake. Before the first fires arrive, the clear-cutting. This culling, they say, is natural. The trees don't shout in pain. But we do not recognize anymore where we are standing. Bold, the contours of the earth exposed, though my favorite path to the upper meadow has been erased. The crowns blaze orange on the hilltop, and we mistake them for the coming dawn. We are new students come for the disorientation. It will be a relief when the needles fall, the space between green crowded with the shadow-limbs of death, blending in, stepping back, the way we are used to it.

THE WOUNDED BIRD

In order of least shyness: evening grosbeak, junco, pygmy owl. When
the pine siskins come, they will be shameless. The bats have their
holocaust in their Vermont caves. The pines die from pine beetles on
our slopes. Some presences are not blessings; they are self-contained,
invitations to investigate further, or warnings to stay away, or
inscrutable, unreadable as a god is. You there, mountain chickadee, in
the thicket, then hopping up my leg. You were struggling, off balance.
You could flutter but not fly, a wobbling presence come out of the
blue. As if you knew I would understand this as approval. Look, I
have always been uneasy using the word god. It has no wind to it,
like you do. It sounds like clod, self-satisfied, a fat man in an overbuilt
house. A period, not a comma, which has wings. I kept returning to
the window until you disappeared into the dusk. Then, nothing could
lighten my mood.

MOON OF THE VISIBLE NESTS

They emerge, each wearing a particular northern costume, construct of spiderweb, lichen, and twilight, inevitable approach of snow, inner moss, tail, pine stick, the all-important grasses. Here is a cup nest with three knitted strings that knot it to a branch of aspen. This one is sloppy and wooden, birthplace of the jays. Their parents have ceded my yard to them. What if we could sleep in it, hung under the night stars, a language of lineage rather than explanation? To go beyond the fascination of what language does—fibers glistening, what the light read of rain. Does the linguist ever mention embroidery? Two sisters, within hours of each other, put themselves to sleep by remembering the blueprint of their grandparents' house, starting at the parlor, the screen always slammed, and ending at the intimate attic door. The whole earth is nest now, with whatever is at hand, mud-paste and twig kick about. We have to watch closely. Concentrate on that. Not on the fact that they have left.

FROSTED MARSH

Marsh-grass like a bank creature, black-footed and salt-tipped. Twilight in the water grown tinsel. You're drawn to them heavily, a clarity stilled, waiting for the body to catch up. No more events, parties, no more running ahead but here with the fever, with what is wrong. The evenings will be long. You will be alone and scared. This familiar out-of-season, not of harvest but of fast, thrift and reticence, faced with the same flaws. Look, the ghosts are calling. Will you ignore them this time? The moat inside midnight blue—your favorite crayon color as a child—sinking, not your favorite, not like breakthrough. To deepen. What does that mean? Earth come down now from sky. Chocolate so rich it has the taste of dung. Will you emerge again, chilled and flowerless, in your hands the dim lamp? Or will you brave an intimacy with something new?

THE BRIDGE

Frost: hair-trigger switch in the middle of the night. Path strewn with pinecones, the blackened leaves of willow. Friend at her chain-link fence, waving to us as we go, the look in her eye already distant. I wish there were a gentler bridge, made of stone pitted by rain that carves a basin midway in which we could place flowers. Sometimes a season widens. We don't need to pick a door. The river lengthens into its horizon, a gradual downward slope. Yesterday, I found myself thinking about hell. If there is such a place, I hope the evil are held there in someone's arms and treated tenderly for the sacrifice of their good lives. I come to the crossing with September in store. What it sees, I see. Time alone to still the self, small beast troubled by controlling winds. The way always one way, back or in.

CROSSING THE WINTER DREAM

I've hit the row of cottonwood, dry and soft, blond and brown with knots of rot and twisted sinews, a tree that does not grow straight but reacts to attacks from the weather, unlike pines, which grow immaculate from their centers out. Before dawn, my windows are frosted. The light at the bird altar gleams. What do we wish when we wish someone good dreams? A bridge, by which I see a crossing, ice palace world with its lavender rim. The anthropomorph in the pictograph looked like an animal from within, its neck elongated, its legs bandied, its head crowned with two horns, slim and striped like an impala's. Out of Africa, out of origin, they spread out. If there were a kind of wood for every emotion, a seasonal myth for the rain-box or savannah bear, it would mean: *Don't worry. Keep going. Everyone drives through it.*

TRANSLATION

The Greeks used the word "translate" to talk of the gods whisking mortals away, to a land not in this world but also not in hell, where they live, not dead, but far removed. Yesterday, walking, I startled two blue grouse. Grouse rising: the sound of snow's collapse. I am sorry I flushed them, though at least they're not the bats, whose hearts slow from a flutter to fifteen beats a minute over weeks, in which case, they might die to wake so fast. Entering into torpor—marmots, snakes, and toads. Mouse-hold, a pocket swept into a surface. I think about the deer I never see, out at night, leaving tracks, the white on white cross-stitch of their feeding. Chickadees, who survive the cold by shivering. Some knowledge resonates; some remains closed, as if the right words weren't chosen. The flower seed dreams on its side and revives, so much of its translation behind it.

MOVING PICTOGRAPH:
PARENTHETICAL SIGNS OF SPRING

In the winter twilight, below the mountain—violet, aqua—the brown prairie unrolls in bolts of suede. The snow patches gather and disperse like herds. The mythic snow deer is what we say. One sole bluebird detaches itself from the sky, that trick most wild things play, which enables us to see the hundred more. The clouds, frothy and wild, tossing their manes and tails, prepare for what they will be: tomorrow. Goatsuckers and swifts. Nightjars and nighthawks. Two false eye spots, high rattle or trill. All things cryptically colored. Like the lynx in the ditch you have longed to see all your life. Like the reindeer. Like the shaman. An animal runs across the road, dives into the ditch, its ears like the forked and broken tines of dogwood. This is the important point: where vision came. And also, at the same time, the vision.

III.

If you would learn the earth
as it really is, learn it through
its sacred places.

N. SCOTT MOMADAY

THE MISSOURI BREAKS

Some things should be seen at a distance: plains cottonwood in their river row, the only tree for miles. The arabesque of white pelicans, each large as a child, one facing downstream, one feeding up. The wind stops when we are not pushing against it. The sky is covered by one plain cloud. We drift, our boats together, your wrist our only hinge. Backwards. Sideways. Past the bank of silver mint and the bright thorns. What message? What duty? The figures of Virgelle sandstone, the volcanic dikes and sills, have emerged on either side of us over millenniums. *Rock face resting between forms.* To get too close is to lose sight of them: the row of tall robed women, the perched, staring eagles, the climbing child, the slow turn they accomplish when they sense us. Into bisque-colored river. Into unglazed statuary of the shore.

TRAVELING PETROGLYPHS: EAGLE CREEK

What does it mean that we are seeing them, that they have left the wall? Left the wall with their spears, hence, before the bow and arrow, with their horns and beaks and tails, with their points and their enhancements—god-shapes grown into the shale, bird-shapes we lure with our eyes, silence the dead wear, with its deep folds. The air is heavy with clay smell. We clap our hands to scare away snakes. And though the sun is bright, hot, it is in memory. Impossible to not see this landscape as one of ruined temples. Sandstone altars. Hoodoos. Pedestals and pillars. That we are here enshrined in earth, an earth of shrines. What is it that we recognize in them? A body, not a plant, something emerging, crudely formed, and yet with presence. Which people this valley of bone.

MADISON BUFFALO JUMP

Snow collects in the creases so that the oldest trails are marked, suddenly visible in the lengths of yellow foothills. To feel oneself into a place the way the pale grasses feel themselves into their long fading from fall. Snow so dry it crumbles into pebbles. We are safe now, the soldiers far gone to their cold beds, the rattlesnakes asleep under warm earth. Only us and the ghosts, who are forgiving and soft, as if we have been allowed to enter time here before the curse. Shoshone first, then Salish, later the Blackfeet, and the Cree, and if we speak, it is in a whisper, pointing out what we almost see, the body permeable, breachable, with pores. If we knew we would be given only one day to be on earth, it would dazzle us so we couldn't breathe. Wind bites our uncovered faces on the climb up to the cliffs, but is mysteriously gone where we expect it strong. Then the creatures fall out of us. The buffalo falls out of us.

PICTOGRAPH: THE FALLING BUFFALO

Finger-pads pawed the crusted stone, wetted with ochre and tallow, smeared finger-lines to bind them, as if the side that were alive needed contact with the other half. Here in our beds, covered with wool, and there, the stars. We, who were once rock, are moving now, though we are supported by bone. We, road-weary and indoors in our minds, the indoor mind, the social one, worried about others. The finely painted buffalo is drawn upside down, which could signify that it is dead. Or, caught in the vortex of trance, what the painter might have made of the electric register. *We were grazing, then running, then the ground, which is all we know, suddenly opened up and betrayed us.* Violence of hard earth. The massive heaviness of the others. Body count, the oldest count of all.

THE GROUND, WHICH IS ONLY HEAVY WIND

The women of the interior prepare themselves for pain by igniting small piles of fir needles on their wrists. I, too, want to age in the mountains, though all my life, I have avoided the extreme. When I turn away in public from the women with white hair, I become less public presence. To stumble on time: the biographic tradition, rift in the concrete I hit with my boots. I have been traveling away from home. I must return to it. Buffalo are the animals women were taught to emulate. They take care of their young. They mate for life, not like the deer, who are flighty and promiscuous. What causes the winds? I thought I knew until today when I distinctly felt them as earth's breath. Hours of shade, grass flattened by early snow, everything tending toward heaviness or lightness. What would we do in this big house alone? How could we possibly keep it?

THE DIFFERENCE BETWEEN LONELINESS
AND SOLITUDE

You think they are opposite, that loneliness is incomplete. How fitting to have the conversation here. Walking atop Ulm Pishkin, snow dust streaming completely down, land empty though never lonely for rain. The Blackfeet believe that anything that casts a shadow is alive. Raven call, but mostly silence, filled with that metallic ring I sometimes think is sky but often is my own blood pressure in my ears. Solitude: our histories, our families wrap the willows in pink light, enlarge the room with a gesture of their far hands. I think I am lonely. Do I have enough buffalo in store? Snow struggles through the sharp-etched particles of air. But what is the difference between solitude and isolation? Last winter, I was busy. This winter, I talk to you. I tell you solitude contains loneliness as a sweetener.

PETROGLYPH: THE HOOFPRINT TRADITION

Thirty thousand years ago, the day was made of ash, powdered bone, fat, and soil, then fired, and fern-like shapes became thoughts. Delicate doe-prints, pretty stamps into the snow—their congregation a crisscross of the social. When did danger enter? Dog tracks (snowflakes), horse tracks (long-legged birds), boots (heavy and nationally patterned). Since the trees have died, trucks have infiltrated the mountains. The rib cages of six deer dumped beside the road. Boulders white with the droppings of feeding ravens. An anthropologist writes that the so-called weapons drawn on cave walls might instead be plants, periodicities of a female sky. Hooves, sliding under it, with horns. Humans, as we had always been, peripheral to the great herds. Their hoofprints, gouged and wind-rocked in the rocks.

THE BLACK CALF

The black calf wakes into a world it has no memory of: adamantine, February cold. Above it, a coarse blue. Into a feedlot with hundreds of others. To wake, one is fortunate. But to have been awakened, to *have been born*, bleary-eyed, stunned, and slick with mucus. Suddenly, a heifer's water breaks. We watch her walk the yard. Agitated, she lies down, lowing. Then up in one motion, and the birth sac drops, long and thin like spittle that soon takes on dimension. Through ghost-cloth the calf's limbs poke out. All premonition, they say, is of terror. To have a body, to be an animal, is muddy business, shit and hay. And bloody afterbirth we see another cow eating. We have a limited number of years to explore the earth, to know predawn, undergrowth in shadow. Noon in its clean lines. Within minutes, the black calf tries to stand.

EAGLE TREE

Their deep brown blackness, their car-length wings. Above a pen of birthing cows, waiting for the afterbirth. That night, I dreamt its weight, a wet cashmere. *A description is not a birthday*, Gertrude Stein writes, yet a flame can turn a morning blue, milk-light in the ruts, its river perhaps the loveliest of rivers. Backlight of winter, foreshadow of spring. Off there, at the edges, something coming. A deer, then a person, then the tracks through snow we made ourselves, lace of ice where the water pools before the dam. How did the eagles know that the cows, the bare cottonwood were here? To know must feel like hunger. It must taste good, you said, viscous and warm, too heavy, ultimately, for them to fly with it. Maybe we're not significant. Undershadow of so much pain. An origin, a destruction we play no part in. The valley soaked and darkened with continuous rain. The eagles waiting above us, undisrupted.

THUNDERBIRD

An old shamanic practice is to concentrate on the body of a mountain, a tree, until one becomes that mountain, that tree. The body of the mountain (weathered). The body of the tree (diseased). Lately when I breathe, I can almost feel breast feathers tugging. When I run, my arms open wide. Solitary, for the most part. Wings—not what you'd think. A heaviness I must lift from the grime. The mind begins to soften its hold on the earth. I call it first forgetting, then dementia. Father and mother moving away from me, to their other home, that of age, and my friends sunk in losses, losing passion. To have had a hard life, what does that mean? To be stuck in one's body, looking outward, away from the clay shack? One harms oneself by thinking that. The eagle is shrewd, aware even of the bad things. Land is the memory spot, sugar. All else is too-brightness, where the soaring fits.

THUNDER EGG

Tunneled out of a volcano, ash-colored and hard, gritty as if fired in a kiln, yet not warm like pottery, cold like a rock, not hollow, rather dense, knocked about. The rock merchant says he finds them tumbled in a stream, but stream rocks are smooth, as is their element. I bought it because I suspected there was a geode inside, a tin and silver amphitheatre like in my dream. Floor sharp-edged, for which I was given sandals. Molten core underneath the earth here, the epicenter close. Red lake. Hot blood and a heart. I wanted it to be relic, from when animals had power, when they cracked out of their shell into the world. Inside this mud-ball, as if shaped by human hands, is not jewel but plain field, resembling calico. What earth makes of her things, devoid of water. But when mixed, lightning. When mixed, the animals, the images begin to form.

THE PHENOMENOLOGY OF FIRE

I remember closing the blinds, noting that I rarely do, as if willing myself to blindness. I remember listening to the wind and hearing objects fall that I did not go out to see, willing deafness. I tightened myself into the house. Criminal, speeding, row song for the time and place, and even then I didn't think of the ashes. I thought adrenalin, its invasion, its purpose and resolve, seeing snow but not stars, hearing the shed collapse. It's a motor that I hear in the image of the fire, though I couldn't have heard it inside—sucking its fuel, an emergency respondent. Blackbirds falling right out of the skies while we lobby for still more concealed weapons. If we still believed in shamans, their task might be too large, to mediate between the village and the weather. Communion at the interior: earth with its core of flame. Over six thousand miles to its center.

PAST LIFE WITH WOOLLY MAMMOTH

Drought, the true sister of bone, carries bone in her arms, as fossils, as skeletal remains. How can the soul's memory remember this? We walk the land, a dun center. Empty, like a scraped-out bowl. Mud puddles and mudslides after the recent, meager snow, churning up animal-shapes in the ravines. What is consciousness? A huge question, fundamental as sandstone or the heavier shale. Ten thousand years ago, the glaciers melted, and now the coal's for sale. Strong winds break in the line of Norwegian poplars. Out of pocket, the stone deposits across the plains. It is a feeling, as in leaves falling, of being left behind, of no longer struggling to hold onto them. To hold onto one's form, is that so important? We went to an ancient sea, you say. The deer browsed the autumn acorns. We were dive-bombed by drunken robins. We went hand in hand through time. The buffalo dozed in the fenced and frozen hayfield.

POWDER RIVER BATTLEFIELD

I know this country, its hundred miles of grasslands and sage, how it can plant its emptiness inside us, separate from our trade, stilled by the profound nature of what happened. Yellowhills. Color as path of cognition. Life here, not covered with dust. What could be more gold than this? I have entered the valley where the dinosaurs lived. Why not call it willow? Dark brown alder flowers against new leaves. Tree people. Rock people. The Christians burned the fields. What kind of fields must they be, hidden with their saved gods. The earth spoke to us. It was frightening. It will be frightening again. All the great cultures know this. How they sang from their own hunger, calling out like dead men, decoys. They whistled for the buffalo who had fled. By what means are they able to come to us? What means of ours keep them away? A teacher's body rotting in a shallow grave—we dismiss the past, thinking we are done with it.

QUESTIONING THE DEAD

Look how they go on without us, how they already existed when we arrived. On the other side, I have learned to say, but they're not somewhere else, they're here, in the green haze about the limbs, between me and that row of cottonwood barely budding. Like the culvert I came to yesterday, the backwater still. I saw what I usually see: the shoreline, the surface, not the upside-down trees, which then swayed into being, though darkly. What is the nature of the eye's adjustments? Take this valley, for instance—where would the dead be? If I hung cloth on the limbs, would they lift it? At what stage do we lose our precious names? Our symptoms? Our traceries? Our handicaps? Our turns of phrase? The shadows we lug everywhere, like an overfull valise? Earth the cool clay tablet where we set it down. I have been wrong to confront them so directly, to stare into the photographs of their battlegrounds.

Spring snow comes softly into the tiny mountain town, from the canyons, which have already turned opaque. A church bell is ringing, anachronistically. No suicide bombs, no gang rape, no nuclear winter, no drone strikes, no polar extinctions. Just a village buried in inconsequence. As if it were a dream we can't re-enter. In the beginning, the authors say, the world was black and white, before the clay wrapped itself around itself, forming an inside and outside. Hole in the bedrock where the water breaks. Dear Sister Outsider. Our Lady Underground. Atmosphere, a ripped frock the shade of swans. We know the soul can become unbalanced, out of tune like a guitar, that snakes and rats will leave their holes when they sense disturbance in earth's core. What does calm say, sinking into its dark-skinned ditch? What does peace say, in the continuous line-making of its horizons? What does oil say, the figure we have chosen for our voice?

PETROGLYPH: CASTLE GARDENS

Late morning, strange, a kind of music. I was in love with earth again. I wanted to stay forever as with a Person. Corridors of sandstone, the white, orange-rose. A flour batter poured into sloping pans that overflow into a sphere larger, more varied than we can travel. There was color where there is no color, inside the abraded circles and incised lines, only a fugitive green or violet, resembling fresco. Like the wash of lilac through the mind when one says *lilac*. Or shadow limbs between real limbs a painter sketches in space only to suggest the complications of lineage. Because there were no horses yet, the walk must have taken weeks, a hundred miles through sage and rabbit bush, far from water and trees. The ground friable, like stepping on wetted ash. They must have set alive a fragrance burning. To prepare their ancestral homeland. To pace themselves inside the dream. That we might have at one time added something to it.

ROCKSLIDE

Once, it must have tumbled down the mountain from the opposite
side, across the creek, with others, in chaotic disruption. Walking late
afternoon, then evening, with a stick against the dogs, I am surrounded
by that event, its particles, en masse, its particular *philopatria* of the
eternal. Moment that lasts until now. I realize this is the condition:
one must stop and ask. If one wants to do this work, under the flux of
passing. We move through the world with a slightly shorter lifespan
than the trees, so perhaps this is why they take our hands. The rock
does not answer, but it slows me, as does the stick tapping on ice, so
that the last mile is at a human pace, which is by foot. We do not yet
know what the dead are. One might call this life. A quiet, a welcome
coming from the water, the sky. Rock, at the bottom, beginning it.

INVISIBLE PETROGLYPH

No animals in sight, only a hawk, one raven, a handful of sage sparrows. Nature loves to hide, Heraclitus wrote. Death hides from us, too, so it must be natural. We say, "she is dead," in present tense, as if it were a form of identity. Where is your mother now? Where will she be tomorrow? We look out over the miles of prairie, painted in monochromatic waves—yellow ocher of the seedpods, charcoal of the volcanic seams—and doubt that they could ever have been magma. You say perhaps this was all seabed, hard to believe in this dry land, only *artemisia* in its many forms, the sparrows tied to it. The earth lives and dies, by which I mean it is completely changed. Like death, time is too much for us. We followed the hearse down the back roads in slow procession past the farm, snow muffling the sound of tires so we were no longer driving but afloat. Not really floating but being moved to some end.

Grateful acknowledgment is made to the editors of the following journals in which some of these poems, sometimes in different versions or with different titles, first appeared:

Bellingham Review: "The Sentience of Rocks," "Moon of the Visible Nests"

Cutbank: "Pictograph: The Red Deer Place," "The Cloud Exercise," "The Crux of Weather Changing"

Flyway: Journal of Writing and the Environment: "The Emerging Field of Image Theory," "The Wounded Bird"

Gettysburg Review: "Sign with Convergent Nested Elements," "Counting the Senses," "The Heron Rookery"

MANOA: "Pictograph: Star Being Cave," "Madison Buffalo Jump," "Cave System," "Pictograph: Hellgate Canyon," "Powder River Battlefield"

The Offending Adam (online: http://www.theoffendingadam.com): "Petroglyph: Bird with Speech Symbol," "Lost Pictograph," "My Pictograph"

Orion (printed under "Rock Drawings of the Northern Plains"): "Petroglyph: The Hoofprint Tradition," "Pictograph: The Falling Buffalo," "Traveling Petroglyphs: Eagle Creek," "Pictograph: Possible Shield-Bearing Figure"

Poetry International: "Kayak," "Petroglyph: the Blue Hare," "Outside the Little Cave Spot," "Geography Lesson"

Prairie Schooner: "The Ross Giant Cedars"

Superstition Review: "The Bridge," "Crossing the Winter Dream," "The Ground, Which Is Only Heavy Wind," "Translation"

Terrain: "Past Life with Woolly Mammoth," "The Missouri Breaks"

Whitefish Review: "Being Quartz," "The Shaman's Cave"

Willow Springs: "Pictograph: The Bird Site, Maze District," "My First Ermine," "Pictograph: Bizarre Anthropomorph with Interior Body Decorations," "The Phenomenology of Fire," "Pictograph: Avalanche Mouth"

"Past Life with Wooly Mammoth" along with "What Does Calm Say" also appeared in *The Petroleum Manga* by Marina Zurkow, edited by Valerie Vogrin and published by Peanut Books (2013), an imprint of punctum books.

A "chapvelope," designed and published by Andrew Wessels of *The Offending Adam*, included "My Pictograph."

A broadside of "Frosted Marsh" was published by North River Press, April 2011. Thank you to Ray Amorosi, editor.

A broadside of "A Talk of Windows" was published by Michigan State University, January 2012. Thank you to Anita Skeen.

I would like to thank Ed Roberson, and the Poetry Society of America, for awarding me the 2009 Alice Fay di Castognola Prize for a work in progress. My gratitude also goes to the Montana Arts Council for granting me The Artist's Innovation Award in 2010, which helped in the completion of this manuscript. The Artist's Innovation Award is made possible by the Montana Arts Council, an agency of State Government, through funding from the National Endowment for the Arts.

The title of the poem "The Ground, Which is Only Heavy Wind" is taken from a line by A.R. Ammons, in his book *Garbage*: "I can't believe / I am merely an old person: whose mother is dead, / whose father is gone and many of whose / friends and associates have wended away to the ground, which is only heavy wind."

The italicized lines in "What Starlight Has Become in the Moving Trees" are from "Relief" by Richard Miles, which appears in *Boat of Two Shores*

My love and gratitude to Rusty Morrison for her faithful literary and spiritual attention to these poems, to Robert Baker, preceptor, translator, correspondent, *companion of the flame*, and to Bryher Herak, always, for traveling with me to the pictographs, both exterior and interior, for her vision and her heart.

Melissa Kwasny has written five previous collections of poems, including *Reading Novalis in Montana* and *The Nine Senses*, which contains a set of poems that won the Poetry Society of America's 2009 Cecil Hemley Award. She also received the Alice di Castognola Award, judged by Ed Roberson, for an early draft of this book.

Melissa Kwasny currently resides in Montana.

Book design by Mary Austin Speaker
Typeset in Joanna MT

Joanna is a transitional typeface designed in the early 1930s by the English sculptor and type designer Eric Gill, and named after one of his daughters.

Printed in the USA
CPSIA information can be obtained
at www.ICGtesting.com
JSHW080005150824
68134JS00021B/2298

9 781571 314628